Rocks and Minerals

Table of Contents

Getting Started 2
Rocks and Minerals 4
Kinds of Rocks 6
Who Studies Rocks? 13
Index 16

by Wiley Blevins

Getting Started

Rocks are all around us. You might find rocks near your home, at the beach, or at the playground.

Some of these rocks may be big enough to sit on. Others may be small enough to hold in your hand.

Did you know that Earth is a huge ball of rock? Earth's rock is broken up into **layers**. The picture on page 3 shows a special view of the inside of Earth. This way, you can see the different layers. Let's take a closer look!

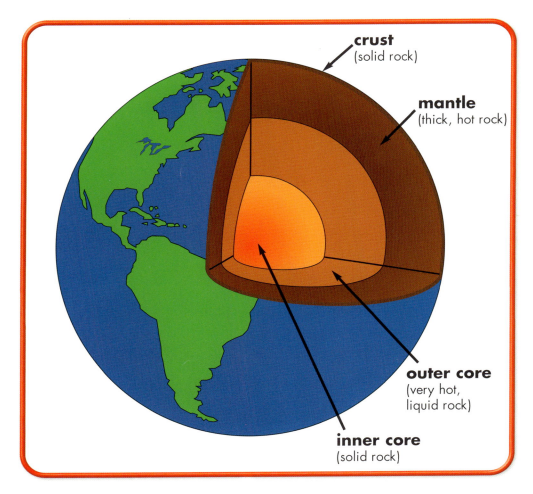

The top layer is called the *crust*. It is like Earth's skin. It is solid rock. Now look at the other layers. How is the rock different in each layer?

Rocks and Minerals

Not all rocks are the same. Some rocks may be shiny and smooth. Some rocks may have many colors.

Even though rocks may be different, they have something in common. Every rock is made up of minerals. In fact, most rocks are made up of more than one mineral. Rocks are formed by minerals joining together.

There are many different minerals in the earth. People use these minerals in many different ways.

Some minerals are made into jewelry.

Salt is a mineral. Gold and silver are minerals, too. So are diamonds and rubies. We get salt and other minerals by mining them, or digging them up from under the ground.

Kinds of Rocks

There are three kinds, or classes, of rocks. The name of each class tells how the rock was made.

Igneous rocks are the hardest and oldest rocks. The word *igneous* means "fire." Igneous rocks start out as hot, melted rock deep under the ground. This hot, melted rock is called *magma*.

Sometimes magma comes up through cracks in Earth's crust. This may happen when the magma pushes up through an opening in a **volcano**. Magma often comes out as hot **lava**. Then it cools and hardens to form igneous rocks.

Lava flowing from a volcano

Sedimentary rocks are the softest rocks. These rocks are formed from something called *sediment*, or small bits of old rocks.

Water and wind cause rocks to break into small bits. The bits get washed into streams and lakes. Then these bits pile up at the bottom of the stream or lake. Sometimes pieces of shells and sand get mixed in. Over time, the **pressure** of the water pushing down on the rock bits causes them to form into solid rock.

There are many different kinds of sedimentary rocks. Two of these are coal and limestone.

One kind of limestone that students and teachers may use is chalk. The next time you use chalk, remember this: Chalk takes millions of years to form!

Metamorphic rocks are formed in a special way. The word *metamorphic* comes from a very old word that means "to change."

Metamorphic rocks start out as sedimentary rocks or igneous rocks. Then something special happens. The rocks are heated by the earth or squeezed under Earth's crust. This causes the rock to change into another kind of rock. For example, limestone is a sedimentary rock. It is soft. When it is squeezed under Earth's crust, it turns into marble.

A statue made from marble

Marble is a metamorphic rock. Marble is very hard. Builders often use marble as a building material. Besides being very hard, marble can be very beautiful! It is often used to make statues and monuments.

This chart gives examples of rocks and some of the ways these rocks are used.

Kinds of Rocks

Igneous Rocks	Sedimentary Rocks	Metamorphic Rocks
Basalt (roads)	Coal (fuel for heating)	Marble (monuments, statues, buildings)
Granite (buildings, curbstones)	Limestone (chalk, cement, buildings)	Slate (roof tiles)

Who Studies Rocks?

A rock can "tell a story." Scientists can learn a lot of information by looking closely at a rock. They can learn how the rock was made. They can learn what the rock is made of. They can also learn what Earth was like when the rock was formed.

The scientists who study rocks are called **geologists**. Besides studying rocks, some geologists may choose to study other parts of Earth—soil, mountains, rivers, oceans, and more.

Many other people are interested in rocks, too. Some people like to collect and study rocks as a hobby. These amateur (AM-uh-chur) rock collectors are also known as "rock hounds"!

It's amazing how much rocks can tell us. This rock, like all rocks, has a long and exciting story. Would you and your classmates like to be rock hounds? Would you like to learn what story a rock might tell?

Index

basalt, 12

chalk, 9, 12

coal, 8, 12

crust, 3, 6, 10

Earth('s), 2–4, 6, 10, 13

geologists, 13

granite, 12

igneous rocks, 6, 10, 12

inner core, 3

layer(s), 2, 3

limestone, 8–10, 12

magma, 6

mantle, 3

marble, 10–12

metamorphic rocks, 10–12

mineral(s), 4, 5

outer core, 3

"rock hounds," 14, 15

sedimentary rocks, 8, 10, 12

slate, 12

volcano, 6, 7